Alfred Seelye Roe

The Old Representatives' hall, 1798-1895

An Address Delivered Before the Massachusetts House of Representatives

Alfred Seelye Roe

The Old Representatives' hall, 1798-1895
An Address Delivered Before the Massachusetts House of Representatives

ISBN/EAN: 9783743411005

Manufactured in Europe, USA, Canada, Australia, Japa

Cover: Foto ©Suzi / pixelio.de

Manufactured and distributed by brebook publishing software
(www.brebook.com)

Alfred Seelye Roe

The Old Representatives' hall, 1798-1895

FREDERIC T. GREENHALGE.
Governor, 1894 —

The Old Representatives' Hall, 1798-1895.

AN ADDRESS

DELIVERED BEFORE THE

MASSACHUSETTS HOUSE OF REPRESENTATIVES,

JANUARY 2, 1895,

BY

ALFRED SEELYE ROE

OF

WORCESTER.

BOSTON:
WRIGHT AND POTTER PRINTING CO., STATE PRINTERS,
18 POST OFFICE SQUARE.
1895.

JANUARY 2, 1895.

Mr. ROE of Worcester offered the following order : —

Ordered, That when the House adjourns to-day it be to meet to-morrow at 11 o'clock A.M., in the chamber set apart for the House of Representatives in the State House Extension, and that hereafter that be the place of meeting.

After remarks by Mr. ROE, the order was adopted, and, on motion of Mr. GROVER of Canton, the thanks of the House were extended to Mr. ROE for his address, and the remarks were ordered to be printed and suitably bound as a House document.

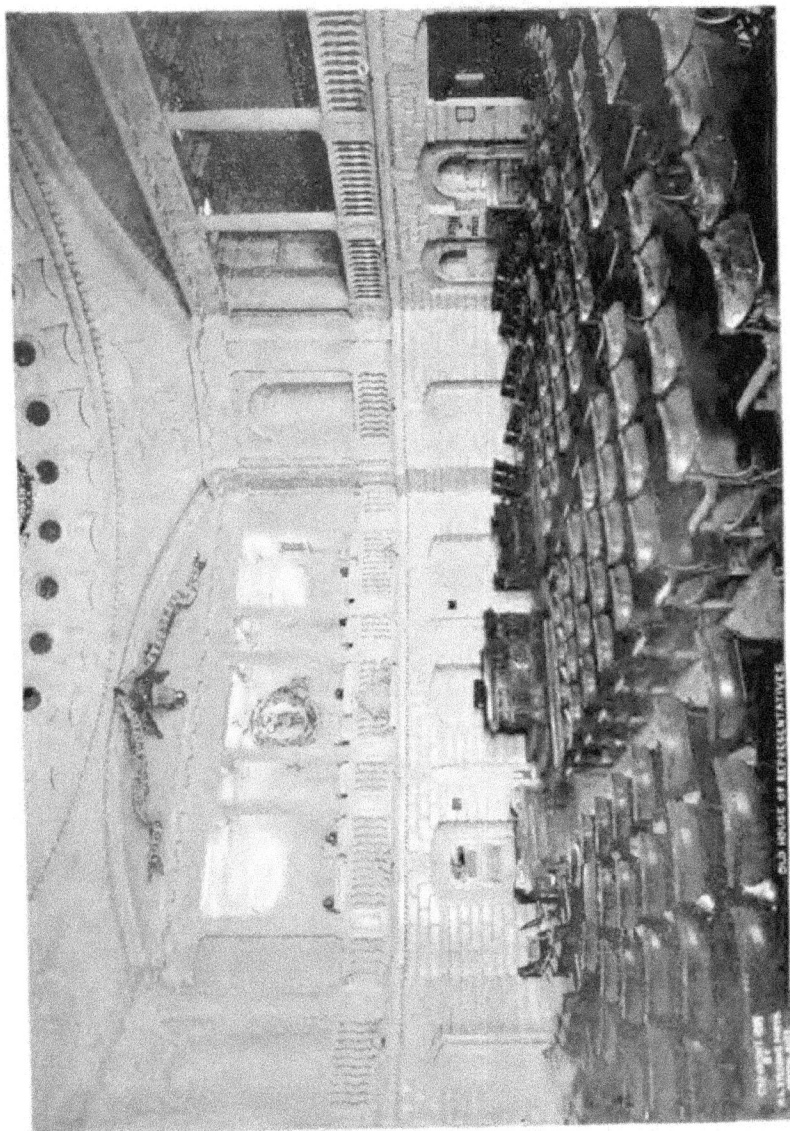

REPRESENTATIVES' HALL — Jan. 2, 1895.

(Looking North.)

ADDRESS.

MR. SPEAKER AND GENTLEMEN OF THE
HOUSE OF REPRESENTATIVES : — While a new
chamber, resplendent with gilt and marble, awaits
us, a place adorned by all that fancy could depict
and art apply, yet it must witness the passing of
a century ere it gathers the interest that attaches
to this hall which we are about to leave. And
now, when our departure is at hand, it would
seem that the event merited more than the mere
gathering up of our effects and our going hence.
Accordingly, from word of mouth, from books
and from tradition, I have collected data and
incident which, in this parting hour, I submit for
your consideration and as a final tribute to this
place, replete with the memories of a hundred
years.

Ninety-seven years ago one week from next
Friday, or on Thursday, the eleventh day of
January, 1798, the Legislature of Massachusetts
assembled for the last time in the old capitol on

State Street. Agreeably to a vote, taken early in
that day, the members were to march at noon to
the new edifice then completed on Beacon Hill.
The structure that they were leaving had stood
just fifty years from its reconstruction, following
the fire of 1747. The one which they were about
to occupy was to see nearly twice that term of
service. Had the artist of the day depicted the
scene as those worthies, who constituted the executive department and General Court of the
Commonwealth, filed out for their memorable
march, he would have drawn first the dignified
figure of Increase Sumner, and by his side that
of Moses Gill, respectively Governor and Lieutenant-Governor. Near them were the other
executive officers with the Council, and following were the Senators, led by President Samuel
Phillips, and the Representatives, at whose head
was Edward Hutchinson Robbins of Milton. A
large share of these men had seen service during
the war of the Revolution, which was still a com-
paratively recent event. As the season was that
of winter, we may conclude that these gentlemen
took the most direct route to the new edifice; and,
this being the case, they must have walked along

INCREASE SUMNER.
Born Nov. 27, 1746; died June 7, 1799.
Governor, 1797 — June 7, 1799.

what is now Washington Street to School, and
thence up that, across Tremont to Beacon, and so
to their destination. In this journey they passed
few structures standing to-day. Before reaching
the old corner book store, then, as now, on School
and Washington, there were possibly two buildings still in existence; one adjoining the book
store (277 and 279 Washington), the other
farther north, and at present undergoing certain
repairs (235 Washington). On School Street,
three ancient buildings (Nos. 5, 7 and 11), just
west of the store, are apparently nearly as old as
the latter. Of the Province House, which stood
farther south, there is now only a small part of
its rear wall (11 and 13 Province Court), but,
meagre as it is, often sought by him who reveres
the past. King's Chapel is, as it was, a silent
witness of the mutations of more than a century.
Whatever there may have been in the way of
buildings for the remainder of the journey, certainly nothing continues in our day. But then,
as they neared the front of, at that time, the most
pretentious capitol in America, they could see
plainly, for it was close at hand, the Hancock
mansion, and, remembering how dear to the

Continental president had been the project of
a State House near his dwelling, we may imag-
ine many a sturdy Representative nudging his
neighbor, as they turned to enter the edifice, and
remarking, "If the old governor had only lived
to see this day!" They had just passed the last
resting place of the patriot and statesman in the
Granary burying ground, where to-day, after
more than a hundred years, his grave has no
adequate memorial.[1] We can fancy the long line
of men filing rapidly through Doric Hall and up
the stairways to this chamber, and occupying, for
the first time, the seats prepared for their reception. It was the winter session of the Legislature of 1797-1798. Speaker Robbins must have
held the gavel, unless he passed it over to
President Phillips.[2] Be this as it may, there
is no doubt that Gov. Increase Sumner, on the
succeeding day, addressed the assembled bodies
in the following words : —

---

[1] The Legislature of 1894 appropriated $3,000 for the purpose of marking
this grave, and proposals for designs have been solicited.

[2] Samuel Phillips, born in North Andover, Feb. 7, 1751; died there, Feb.
10, 1802; Lieutenant-Governor of the Commonwealth at the time. Twenty
years a State senator and for fifteen years president of the Senate, said years
consecutive (1782-1801), except the single year's presidency, in 1787-88, of
Samuel Adams.

GENTLEMEN OF THE SENATE AND GENTLE-
MEN OF THE HOUSE OF REPRESENTATIVES : —
While I rejoice with you, and my fellow citizens
at large, on the completion of this stately edifice,
not less honorable to the Commonwealth, at whose
expense it was erected, than ornamental to the
capital which generously provided the place, permit me to express my entire satisfaction at the
ingenious manner in which the plan has been
executed. Begun and finished in little more than
two years, it exhibits a pleasing proof of the
architecture, skill and fidelity of your agents who
planned and superintended the work, while it
demonstrates the ability of the artificers who
performed it.

Combining the advantages of suitable retire-
ment, a healthy situation and delightful prospect
with such elegant and very convenient apartments
for the security of the records and for transacting
the public business, there is perhaps no public
building to be found within the United States
more useful or magnificent. I am confident that
you, gentlemen of both Houses of the Legislature,
will cordially join me in the fervent wish that this
State House may long remain a monument of the
public spirit of the citizens of Massachusetts, as
well as a testimony of their respect to our happy
political institutions. We will then, under the
smiles of Heaven, unite in dedicating it to the
honor, freedom, independence and security of
our country. In this House may the true principles of the best system of civil government the

world has ever seen be uniformly supported; here
may every practice and principle be successfully
opposed that tend to impair it; here may every
act of the Legislature be the result of cool delib-
eration and sound judgment; and in this House,
on all necessary occasions, may the Supreme
Executive, agreeably to the laws of the land, in
mercy cause judgment to be executed, and each
branch of our elective government continue faithful in the discharge of its trust. God grant that
neither external force or influence, nor internal
commotion or violence, may ever shake the pillars
of our free Republic.

The men thus addressed would have been note-
worthy anywhere, but to us they have a peculiar interest as our predecessors, nearly a hundred
years away. They were only seventeen years
from the close of the Revolutionary war. Among
a people that had sent into the struggle more than
92,000 men it would not be strange if a large per-
centage of the men before us had borne arms in
that immortal strife.[1] It is certain that very few
of those whose names have been borne on the
wings of fame had no part in that conflict. While
some of the leading officers may not have carried

---

[1] Reference to the revolutionary archives discloses that at least ninety-one of
these Representatives had seen service during the struggle for liberty. Many of
them had served throughout the war, attaining, in many cases, high rank.

MOSES GILL.
Born Jan. 18, 1733; died May 20, 1800.
Lieutenant-Governor, 1794 -- May 20, 1800.

muskets, yet in some way they had periled life
and reputation for what they deemed the right.
There were one hundred and eighty-nine members
of the House, and they came from all parts of the
Commonwealth, including the district of Maine.
The town of Lincoln sends her honored son, Capt.
Samuel Hoar, the grandfather of our United
States Senator, Geo. F. Hoar, himself a man who
could tell the story of fighting for fatherland. He
had been one of the party that conducted to the
seaboard the British officers and men captured at
Saratoga. Here, too, is Richard Devens, whose
blood three generations afterwards was to appear
in the person of Charles Devens, soldier and
jurist; and the great-grandfather is a soldier also
— one of the men sent by Charlestown. Among
the Boston members is Dr. William Eustis, who
throughout the war had done efficient service as a
surgeon, and who, a few years afterwards, was to
be governor of the State. Worcester sends down
Levi Lincoln, Sr., for many years an invaluable
holder of State and national office, lieutenant-governor in 1807–1809 and again in 1823–1824. He
had responded as a minute man. And there was
Caleb Strong from Northampton, a man for the

times, bearing in his nature all the qualities indicated in his name, the man who later had the
hardihood to oppose the war of 1812, not because
he was afraid to fight, for he knew the whole
story of the Revolution. He had been Senator in
the national capital, and was to be the very next
governor, in which capacity he had the bravery to
overlook the beruffled gentry of the existing ju-
diciary, and to make Theophilus Parsons chief
justice of the supreme court, an act for which subsequent generations cannot be grateful enough.
As a study of heredity it is interesting to com-
pare the names of these Representatives of a
century since with those of the men last elected
to this body, and I find no less than thirty-eight
coincidences. I cannot state that the members of
to-day are descended from the good men of 1798,
but the surnames continue. Going through the
list, I find Barnes (2), Bates, Bliss, Brown (2),
Clark, Drew, Drury, Holland, Holt, Howe, Hutchinson, Kingman, Mellen (2) (this name suggests
the frequent remark that he, by common consent
yeleped "Jim,"[1] has been in the House so long
that the memory of man runneth not to the con-

---

[1] James H. Mellen, Worcester, thirteen times elected to the House.

trary. Confirmation of this statement is found in the appearance of his name in 1798, though in those days they called him James, and he lived in Holliston), Mitchell, Norton, Parker, Perkins, Phelps, Putnam, Rice, Richardson, Rowe,[1] Russell, Sargent, Smith (2), Snow, Stone, Strong, Thacher, Thurston, Turner, White (2), and Wood. One of the first acts of the House, thus assembled, was to vote the front seats to the Boston members, — a distinction of which the successors of those same members have always thought themselves worthy though they have not in every case secured what they wished. Very likely this courtesy was extended on account of the gift by Boston of the site of the State House.

Owing to the season of the year, it will not seem especially strange that on the first day (January 10), in the old State House, it was voted to expend $150 for the purchase of fuel. The fireplaces of those days, though healthful, were

---

[1] By members of the same family this name is spelled both with and without the w. John Rowe of Gloucester is here referred to. He was for nine years a member of the House from that place, and one year from Essex County in the Senate. He later removed to Milton, where he had inherited at least a portion of the property of his uncle, that John Rowe of Boston at whose instance in 1784 the figure of the codfish was suspended in the Representatives' Chamber of the Old State House.

fearfully voracious. But the chamber now first
occupied had a somewhat different appearance
from that which we know. There were no north
and south galleries, and no addition on the north
side; so those gentlemen, as they took their seats,
had a clear outlook through the north windows to
Bunker Hill, whose history they knew by heart,
and doubtless many a man could have told of
Putnam and Prescott and the events of that immortal 17th of June. There was really no reason
why they should not look away to Bunker Hill,
for there were very few buildings to shut out the
view. Towards the west, and close at hand, they
must have noted the column on the highest part
of Beacon Hill, which was not only a tribute to
the talent and patriotism of Bulfinch the con-
structor,[1] but a fitting memorial to the heroism of
the men of the Revolution, of whom they were a
portion, and towards the history, written on the
tower's tablets, they had contributed no inconsid-
erable part. It was, too, the very hill on which
had stood the beacon for a hundred and fifty

---

[1] On his return from Europe, in 1786, Mr. Bulfinch, impressed with the
desirableness of some memorial of Revolutionary valor and sacrifices, solicited
the funds for this monument, which he designed, and whose construction in 1790
he superintended. It was taken down in 1811.

— from your affectionate Father,
Charles Bulfinch

Born Aug. 8, 1763; died April 15, 1844.
Architect.   Member of Building Commission.

years, ever a hateful sight to tyrants. The figure
of the eagle, which, since 1850, has hung over
the Speaker's head, then surmounted Bulfinch's
tower, and the tablets on the walls of the corri-
dor south of Doric Hall were attached to its base.
After the manner of their British ancestors, these
men sat with covered heads, a custom that prevailed till well along into the thirties.[1]

In those days there was little dallying over
what might be considered liberty of thought, for
every man had been obliged to subscribe to the
following oath: "I, A. B, do declare that I
believe the Christian religion and have firm per-
suasion of its truth." The fact, too, that he
was there, was evidence that he was possessed
of a freehold yielding an annual income of three
pounds, or was possessed of property to the value
of fifty pounds. In addition to the foregoing
oath, all had to renounce all allegiance to the king
or queen of Great Britain and to every other

---

[1] Jan. 6, 1838, George W. Warren of Charlestown introduced an order
instructing the committee on Rules to inquire into the expediency of requir-
ing members to sit with uncovered heads. The order was negatived, but its
introduction indicates the trend of custom. Hats gradually disappeared during the sittings, though the Hon. John I. Baker says many members wore
them in 1840, possibly out of sympathy with the Friends or Quaker members,
who carried into the Legislature the habits of their daily lives.

foreign power whatever : "And that no foreign
prince, person, prelate, state or potentate hath or
ought to have any jurisdiction, superiority, pre-
eminence, authority, dispensing or other power in
any matter, civil, ecclesiastical or spiritual, within
this Commonwealth, except the power which is or
may be vested by their Constitution in the Congress of the United States. And I do further tes-
tify and declare that no man or body of men hath,
or can have, any right to absolve or discharge
me from the obligation of this oath, declaration
or affirmation," etc. Having fought a good fight,
those people were not disposed to put their per-
sons in chancery, at least of their own volition.

Several days after, or the 16th, the House responded to Governor Sumner's address, saying : —

May it please your Excellency : — The House
of Representatives have received your Excellency
with great pleasure in the new and elegant building erected for the better accommodation of the
several branches of government.

In this splendid specimen of the taste and judgment of the agents who planned and superintended, and in the ability of the artificers who
completed its structure, we are happy to find the
public confidence completely justified. Long may
it continue an ornament to the capital, whose

REPRESENTATIVES' HALL— January, 1852.

(Looking North.)

NATHANIEL P. BANKS, Jr., Speaker.

inhabitants generously gave the situation on which it is erected, and a monument of the public spirit of the people of Massachusetts, sacred to the purposes to which it has been devoted.

Thus was inaugurated the ninety-seven years' occupancy of this hall. The story of this period, told in full, fills whole alcoves of the State library. In brief, we have the resultant in the volume of statutes. More than sixteen thousand different men have here acted their parts, long or short. Of course the large majority came for a year only, and thereafter dated all events from the year " I was in the House." While affairs were directed by the few, it was ever a laudable ambition to hold a seat in this chamber. The Legislature of Massachusetts is the oldest continuous legislative body in America, and certainly no other one holds a higher rank in attainments and general worth. "The member from Cranberry Centre" has long been the butt of wit and satire; but take him for all in all, he is a type of whom the world may well be proud. Here were begun the careers that led through the highest honors in the gift of the State and nation. This space is an arena in which many a gladiator has given proof of his metal.

Through this chamber passed every Governor
after 1798, save nine. Of these, two had been
members of the Senate, and two, Morton and
Emory Washburn, came hither long after they
had doffed the robes of executive office, the latter
appearing in his old age to be the dean of the
House and to die while a member. So then,
of the whole thirty-one individuals holding the
highest office in the State, only John Davis,
Edward Everett, George N. Briggs, Alexander
H. Rice and William E. Russell gained their
places save through some service in the Legislature. With our lieutenant-governors the case
is similar. There have been thirty-two of these
officers, and only Elisha Huntington and John
Nesmith failed to see some time in one or both
of the branches of the Legislature. Five, viz.,
Phillips, Goodrich, Weston, Ames and Haile,
were in the Senate only, while Plunkett, Brown
and Trask came back after their higher honors
to wrestle here. Since 1798 thirty-two men have
been United States Senators from this State, and
of these only Pickering, Davis, Everett and Sumner were in neither body; John Quincy Adams,
Prentiss Mellen and Samuel Dexter were in the

ROGER WOLCOTT.
Lieutenant-Governor, 1893 —

Senate; the other twenty-six were, more or less,
in the House and in the Senate also. The same
rule applies to the Representatives in Congress
from Massachusetts. Of the present thirteen
members, only Wright, Apsley, Everett, Draper
and Randall have not been in the House: the
latter has served in the Senate. The importance
of a position here may be gathered from the fact
that in former times it was not unusual for the
same man to be nominated and elected to both
bodies, in which case he had his choice of places.
So experienced and wily a manager and statesman
as Elbridge Gerry never failed to choose the nom-
inally lower House, seeing in it a broader field for
talent and energy. How others, outside of our
numbers, have regarded this body we may learn in
part from the language of that long-time clerk of
the Senate, Stephen N. Gifford, when his friends
were giving him his famous complimentary dinner
in 1882: "Who has made Massachusetts the best
Commonwealth on the face of God's earth but the
Legislature of Massachusetts." That most courtly
of gentlemen and affable of officers, Sergeant-at-
Arms Benjamin Stevens, once became as near
being excited as he was ever known to be over an

indication that a certain governor was endeavoring to influence legislation. Raising his hands in deprecation, he exclaimed, " The idea of any governor attempting to influence the highest power in the Commonwealth of Massachusetts! "

For many years, or till 1858, the numbers constituting this body were variable. From 1780 to 1837, the basis of representation was as follows: Every corporate town having one hundred and fifty ratable polls was entitled to one Representative; those having three hundred and seventy-five could have two Representatives, six hundred ratable polls could have three, and so on, one additional Representative for every two hundred and twenty-five additional qualified voters, provided that every town, then incorporated, though it might not have the requisite number of polls, should not be deprived of representation, but no town could thereafter be incorporated with less than the one hundred and fifty qualified voters with the privilege of representation. The General Court had power to fine a town if it failed to avail itself of this electoral privilege. The system that went into operation in 1837 was, if possible, more cumbersome than that which it

BENJAMIN STEVENS.

Born April 16, 1790; died Feb. 11, 1865.

Sergeant-at-Arms, 1835 — 1859.

displaced. Three hundred ratable polls became the basis for one Representative; any city or town having four hundred and fifty additional voters could have an additional Representative. Where the town had less than the requisite three hundred, the number of polls at the last preceding decennial census was multiplied by ten and the product divided by three hundred, and the quotient indicated the number of times within ten years that the town might elect one Representative. The same plan prevailed with the excess above the required number in cities and towns already entitled to one Representative, with this difference, that here the product of excess multiplied by ten was to be divided by four hundred and fifty. The result, to the Solons who devised this scheme, must have been surprising, for they had set out to reduce the numbers of their House, in 1837, consisting of six hundred and thirty-five members. It had been evident that something must be done, for a House so numerous, became, surely, too popular a branch. The next year, under the new rule, the number dropped to four hundred and eighty, but in 1839 and 1840 it went up to five hundred and twenty-one. Accordingly

a new plan was again devised, and now the basis
of representation is to be twelve hundred inhabitants, quite a step upward, and twenty-four hundred is the mean advancing number to increase
the representation. Where there are less than
twelve hundred people the town may elect one
Representative as many times in every ten years
as one hundred and sixty is contained times in the
number of inhabitants, and such towns may elect a
Representative for the year in which the valuation
of estates within the Commonwealth is settled.
At this time comes the beginning of the forma-
tion of legislative districts from adjoining towns,
with all the privileges with reference to representation accorded to a town having the same
number of inhabitants. To provide for the inevitable increase of inhabitants, it was further or-
dained that whenever the population of the State
should reach seven hundred and fifty thousand,
the number that should entitle a town to a Representative, the mean increasing number which
should entitle a town to more than one, and also
the number by which the representation of towns
not entitled to a Representative every year is to
be divided shall be increased, respectively, by one-

GEORGE V. L. MEYER.
Speaker, 1894 —

tenth of the numbers above mentioned. Whenever seventy thousand people are added to the
population, one-tenth shall again be added, as
before. As all the members of the Governor's
Council during these years had not had the benefit
of full college courses in mathematics, the wonder
constantly grows that at each recurring ten years
there was not a marked addition to the inmates in
the various State lunatic asylums. However, the
people worried along with their variable numbers
in their popular branch till they hit upon the only
feasible solution of their problem, viz., a definite.
constant number, which they decided should be
two hundred and forty. This amendment went
into effect in 1858, and continues to date. The
property qualification went out in the amendment
of 1840. The peculiar oaths prescribed by the
Constitution ceased with the ratification of the
Constitutional Convention of 1820.

The fathers did not vote themselves magnificent
salaries. The very first session in this chamber
rated the services of the public servants at two
dollars per day, and by Constitution they were
entitled to mileage, which they rated at two dollars for every ten miles. This compensation con-

tinued for nearly or quite fifty years. Indeed,
mentioning this subject, our venerable friend,
John I. Baker of Beverly, says that in 1840, his
first year, he boarded at the Pemberton House on
the site of the present Howard Athenæum, and,
though he was in the Legislature when more
liberal salaries were allowed, that was the only
year when he saw a margin in his favor.

There were subsequent rises, till we come to
the pay of to-day, small when compared with the
fifteen hundred dollars paid by New York, yet
making, with the two dollars per mile mileage, a
very large aggregate. The forbidding of railroad
passes to officials of the State was an act of the
Legislature of 1892.[1] In 1832 small clothes disappeared, three members then wearing such in-

---

[1] Feb. 28, 1851, it was voted to permit the drawing of the sum of $50 per
month, provided the pay due amounted to that sum. Feb. 1, 1855, the pay was
raised to $3 per day, and the possible monthly drawing was made $75. Jan. 30,
1858, annual compensation was placed at $300. The mileage of $1 for every five
miles was payable the first day of the session; on the first day of each month
thereafter members could draw $2 per day, and on the final day all arrears
May 14, 1864, the legislators voted themselves an additional $100, and passed the
act over the governor's veto. It was for that year only. June 22, 1870, compensation was set at $5 per day. April 14, 1871, pay was fixed at $750 a year. In
1872 the drawing of $100 per month was permitted. Feb. 29, 1876, the salary
went back to $650 per annum. Feb. 28, 1879, pay reduced to $500. Jan. 29,
1885, pay raised to $650. June 30, 1886, compensation placed at its present
figure, viz., $750.

EDWARD A. MCLAUGHLIN.
Clerk, 1883 —

teguments, one of whom being Maj. Thomas
Melville of Boston tea party fame, and who is
also supposed to have been the last American to
wear the cocked hat. Between small clothes and
the oldest living representative, or the old and the
new, there is no break.

Sessions have varied much in length, though
in later years few have gone under one hundred
and fifty days. The year 1798 beheld the law
makers of Massachusetts in this building eighty-
three days. There have been shorter terms, and
of course many that were longer. The longest
session was in General Butler's year, and it
dragged along through two hundred and six
weary days. The closing chapter in the book
of this chamber had one hundred and eighty
pages. We started in to make a record of
brevity, but our progress was halted, para-
doxically, it would seem, by rapid transit.

Few Massachusetts people of middle life have
not heard of the wonders of 'lection day. Then
the Commonwealth put on her best and saw the
Governor inaugurated. All this was on the last
Wednesday in May. The legislative year began
then, the members having been elected in that

month, with at least ten days intervening. The
summer session was, however, a brief one, seldom
lasting a month. In January they came together
again for their protracted stay, extending occa-
sionally well along towards the dandelion season.
With the proverbial conservatism of the English
race, people who are marvels of inertia, whether
of motion or rest, still seen in the retention of
town meeting in the month of March or April,
simply because the year began in March when the
earlier towns were formed, our State held on to
the old custom till 1832, when it was thought desirable to make the political year conform to that
of the calendar. Gov. Levi Lincoln had the privilege of promulgating the 10th amendment in 1831,
June 15, and he was the first Governor to be inaugurated in the January following; but for fifty
years there were not wanting those who bewailed
the loss of 'lection day.

It has been said that of the making of many
books there is no end; and of the truth of the
statement there would be no doubt were all of us
to see the mass of printed matter that, first and
last, the Massachusetts Legislature has been re-
sponsible for. And the books that have been pre-

NATHANIEL P. BANKS, Jr.

Born Jan. 30, 1816; died Sept. 1, 1894.

Speaker, 1851 — 1852.

served are nearly legion. Then, too, the volumes grow in size. The first product of laws from this Capitol numbered eighty-one folio pages, the last, that of 1894, fills a royal octavo of seven hundred and fifty-six pages. The first Blue Book or Acts and Resolves came in 1839, bound in blue, doubtless because the rules and orders had been thus colored for years.

In the earlier days and even down to a quite recent period members did not think it necessary to take a Saturday recess. Jan. 9, 1877, John D. Washburn of Worcester introduced an order, to the effect that when the House adjourn on Friday it be to meet on the following Monday at two o'clock, until otherwise ordered. Revolutions seldom move backward, and there have been very few Saturday sessions since.

The legislator who to-day rides comfortably a hundred or more miles to and from the daily sessions of the General Court has little notion of the troubles of those who came hither a century since or even in much later days. Then the country member came to stay till the work was done, and he rather liked to labor Saturdays, for it hastened the day of his return. The hills of Berkshire

were three days away, and Washington County,
Maine, much farther. The horse that he may
have ridden to town was pining for the rich
pastures of the home fields, and homesickness
was not an unknown complaint to the Solon himself. It is said that some of these far-away Representatives used to put their steeds out to pasture
in the neighboring towns, and some even disputed
the grassy slopes of the Common with the regular
dwellers in Boston. It is an interesting item that,
when the Messenger's house at 46 Hancock Street
was built, provision was also made for the horses
of the members who rode or drove in from the
nearer towns. There were spaces for between
thirty and forty beasts, and the doors were opened
in the morning by an employee of the Messenger,
and by him closed at night. The Solons were
their own hostlers, as well as Jehus. After a
time the State sold the land thus employed to
the city of Boston, and it was long covered by
the reservoir. Later the State bought it back,
and our new Representatives' Hall is not far
from covering the land where our predecessors
groomed and fed their steeds with grain and fod-
der brought by them from their respective homes.

JACOB KUHN.
Born Nov. 25, 1763; died Sept. 22, 1835.
Messenger, 1786 — 1835.

There have been but five men [1] who as messenger or sergeant-at-arms have had the care of this building. Jacob Kuhn, who came here with the first comers, was for more than fifty years connected with the Legislature. Small in stature, yet he was the soul of graciousness, and was all that faithfulness implies. The first sergeant-at-arms was Benjamin Stevens. A member of this body, he resigned to take the office, which he held for twenty-five years. No one knew his duty

[1] Jacob Kuhn, to 1835; Benjamin Stevens, Boston, 1835-59; John Morissey, Plymouth, 1859-74; Oreb F. Mitchell, Boston, 1874-85; John G. B. Adams, Lynn, 1886- . Jacob Kuhn, born Nov. 25, 1763, in Boston, died there in the messenger's house, on the reservoir site, Sept. 22, 1835. His father was John George Kuhn, born in Königsberg, East Prussia, Aug. 1, 1740, who came to America in 1754, and was for many years a school-master in Boston. He died Nov. 20, 1822. Jacob's grandfather was Jacob, a native of Gochsheim, Würtemberg, who came to this country in 1754 and, with his eldest son, was drowned, Nov. 28, 1763, at the mouth of the Kennebec River, at a place since known as Kuhn's Point. In 1781, Jacob Kuhn became assistant messenger, and in 1786 was advanced to full charge, dying in office in 1835. Of him his son said, "He was strictly temperate, inflexibly honest, unbending in duty, kind, generous, pious and remarkably patient under trials, of which he had a full share." At his death the Legislature voted to have his funeral public in the Representatives' chamber, but the family preferring, it was held privately at his late home, with deputations from the Senate and House attending. He was buried in the family tomb in the old Common Burial Ground.

Benjamin Stevens was born in the city of Boston; was in the House of Representatives in 1833, 1834 and 1835; in the last year he resigned to become the successor of Messenger Jacob Kuhn, being the first to hold the office of Sergeant-at-Arms. He was again elected to the House in 1862, and in 1863, during the absence of Maj. John Morissey, who was serving a nine months' term as major of the 3d Regiment, Mr. Stevens again performed the duties of Sergeant-at-Arms. His body lies in Mt. Auburn. It was during Mr. Stevens' term of office

better, and no one had a wider range of friends.
As an illustration of his tact, the story is told that
a certain gentleman of decayed fortunes had taken
up the habit of walking in Doric Hall. Day after
day he kept up his peregrinations, pausing only to
borrow a dollar of some impressionable country-
man. As the dollar was never paid back, and as
the purses of the members were none too long,
they complained to Mr. Stevens, who in his bland-
est manner requested the walker to take up his

---

that he made Thomas J. Tucker a State House employee. The latter, now the
senior of all those having the Capitol in charge, was born in Boston, Dec. 21,
1831, was graduated from the Mayhew School, and, after a short experience in
business, became a messenger here, Jan. 1, 1856. He was made assistant door-
keeper in 1869, and door-keeper in 1875.

John Morissey was born in Boston, of Irish descent. He was a printer by
trade and as such worked in Nantucket, whence, in 1849, he was sent to the
House and again in 1857. In 1858 he represented the Island District in the
Senate. During the same year he removed to Plymouth, which place was his
home till his death. Coming into office during the administration of Governor
Banks, he served, excepting a term of active military service as major of the
3d Regiment, till long after the Civil War, during which struggle he was of
especial value to Governor Andrew. Returning to his home at the end of his
State House career, he became in 1877 treasurer of Plymouth County, and as
such continued to the time of his death.

Captain Mitchell enlisted early in the War of the Rebellion from the town of
Middleborough. As a captain in the 40th Regiment he lost an arm at Drury's
Bluff, May 16, 1864. He is now a resident of Boston.

Captain Adams served throughout the war in the 19th Regiment. He was
twice severely wounded at Gettysburg, on the second day. In 1864, June 22,
he was captured by the enemy before Petersburg, and was held a prisoner till
March 1, 1865. It will be noted that every Sergeant-at-Arms, save the first, was
a soldier during the Rebellion.

JOHN MORISSEY.
Sergeant-at-Arms, 1859 — 74.

line of march in some new direction; whereupon
the reproved turned upon the officer and fiercely
replied, "Move on! why, I own a part of this
building." "Sure enough, so you do," said Mr.
Stevens, "and when we divide it you shall have
your share." So effectual was the rejoinder that
the part owner disappeared completely. Through
Morissey and Mitchell we come to Captain
Adams, and long may he be the last.

Whether or not service here is conducive to
longevity, it is certain that some members have at-
tained very old age. The senior surviving Representative is Henry Mills, now of Binghamton,
N. Y., but in his legislative days from Millbury.
He served in the Houses of 1833-34. At last
accounts he was hale and hearty, and able to
write a particularly vigorous letter. Joshua T.
Everett of Westminster, though he represented
Princeton in this hall, survives, at eighty-eight
years, a fellow legislator with Mr. Mills in 1834.
Few of the men here to-day step off more nimbly
than does this Worcester County nonogenarian,
who, in November last, told me that on the next
morning he expected to walk over to his old home
in Princeton, nearly six miles distant. Of all

those who have held places here, few if any, in
later years, exceed the term of service of John I.
Baker, long known as the blue-eyed philosopher
of Beverly, and who, at the age of eighty-two, his
newly formed city, by a unanimous vote, makes
her first mayor, by such action honoring herself
no less than her aged citizen. As a member of
the Harbor and Land Commission he still renders
the State valuable service. His first year was
1840, his last 1884; and between them he sat
eighteen years in this chamber.

When he came hither, this room was unchanged
from the shape given it by the builders, with the
possible addition of balcony galleries on each side.
Then light came in at the north windows and from
the south; it streamed in through right-angled
spaces where is now the special gallery. The
two corners at the south had their fireplaces, as
of yore, and daily consumed great quantities of
wood. They admitted of good ventilation, but
real warmth was to be had only by *heated* discus-
sions, which we have reason to believe were not
often wanting. Here in the opposite corners were,
at a slight elevation, private boxes, where the
favored visitors might witness the contests in the

OREB F. MITCHELL.
Sergeant-at-Arms, 1875   1885.

ROBERT C. WINTHROP.
Born May 12, 1809; died Nov. 16, 1894.
Speaker, 1838—1840.

arena. Instead of the chairs known to us of a
later date, were fixed settees extending across the
hall, with certain passageways. The clerk's desk
was in front of that of the speaker, and the large
area in front was filled with movable settees for
the accommodation of members. The latter were
so numerous that they filled the entire floor, both
galleries, and, for their further convenience, balconies had been constructed on each side, affording seats for sixteen men in each one. Mr. Baker
says that, as the names of Texas and Oregon were
often heard in those days, by some queer combi-
nation the west gallery was called Oregon; the
east, Texas; and so dignified a presiding officer as
Robert C. Winthrop would address men in these
places as the member in Texas, or the other place,
as it happened. From the light afforded in the
evening by tallow dips, through the period of gas
to the present system of electricity, the progress
has been marked and desirable. There was no
chandelier till the introduction of electricity. For
many years the House got along well enough with
only one clock, that facing the speaker; but it
remained for Representative Daniels of Oxford,
1877, who sat too far back to derive any good

from the clock, to introduce an order that a time-
piece be placed behind the speaker and in front
of the members, a proposition at which all laughed
and for which a majority voted, and then, when
its convenience was discovered, wondered that no
one had thought of it before. In those days,
the entrances to this hall were near the fireplaces
towards the south, instead of being in the middle
of each side, as now.

The renovation and additions of 1853 very sen-
sibly changed the conditions here. The large
Bryant addition on the north closed the lower
windows on that side, but gave light through
higher ones, and at the same time provided excellent places for the reporters, who before that had
been huddled down by the speaker's side. On the
south there was an extension under the balcony,
affording the much-used passageway and the gallery above, the lower convenience, especially, being
one that the smokers of the Legislature could
hardly spare, though its very existence may have
given origin to the local name of "Murderers
Row," long applied to the last range of seats at
the south. Changes having been begun, subse-

JOHN G. B. ADAMS.
Sergeant-at-Arms, 1886 —

quent ones were effected the more easily; and
in 1866 a very complete overhauling was had,
in which the balconies disappeared, likewise the
fireplaces and the settees, heat being afforded by
a system of furnaces. Though Architect Wm.
Washburn was much criticised by the press and
people for what he did and for what he did not
do, he says, in his report, "The ventilation of the
Representatives' Hall is perhaps the most complete success ever accomplished in this country,"
— an opinion and statement which seem quite
amusing when placed side by side with the many
criticisms heard in recent years.

So much for the material changes. Men have
come and gone. They have here played their
brief parts and have been crowded off. Few
men have achieved political distinction in this
Commonwealth without having been, at some
time, connected with this House. Daniel Webster was a member in 1822, but he did not come
in till the second day, and had to be sworn by
himself. He was not a member of any committee, and the journal has his name only once, and
then as one of a special committee to report at the

winter session a system of rules. I cannot find
that he ever reported.[1] It should be stated, in the
matter of committees, that in the early days there
were only eleven joint standing ones, and of the
House there were eight. This was the case in
Webster's day. In 1835, John G. Whittier had
a seat here from Haverhill, and he was re-elected
in 1836, but illness prevented his taking his place.
The father of Senator Hoar, Samuel Hoar of
Concord, after his term in Congress was a member, and was instrumental in saving the rights
and privileges of Harvard College. The Senator himself was here in 1852. Noah Webster,
the famous maker of the dictionary, represented
Amherst for three years, when the century was
in its teens.

At the clerk's desk for twelve years, or from
1832 to 1843, sat Luther S. Cushing, whose
manual on parliamentary usage has been the
school-boy's Bible for more than fifty years.
As a gentleman has remarked, the Legislature
has had the man who made the dictionary and

---

[1] In fairness to Mr. Webster, it should be stated that, having been elected
to Congress in the autumn of 1822, it is possible that he did not feel obligated
to give any of his subsequent time to the Legislature.

LUTHER S. CUSHING.

Born June 22, 1803; died June 22, 1856.

Clerk, 1832 — 1843.

the one who made the manual, so that there seems to be lacking only the maker of the Bible. Fifteen others [1] link 1798 with 1883, when Edward A. McLaughlin became our efficient clerk.

From Robbins to Meyer, forty-three men [2] have occupied the speaker's chair. Of these, the longest consecutive holding in this chamber was by William B. Calhoun of Springfield, seven years; though Timothy Bigelow, representing Groton

---

[1] In this number should be mentioned the names of William Schouler, 1853, who was adjutant-general during the war period, and who wrote the standard "History of Massachusetts in the Rebellion;" William S. Robinson, 1862–1872, whose caustic pen as correspondent of the "Springfield Republican," while it brought him fame, also made him hosts of enemies; Charles H. Taylor, 1873, long manager of the "Boston Globe;" George A. Marden, 1874–1882, only a year since retiring from the five years treasurership of the State. The first clerk to serve here was Henry Warren, youngest son of Gen. James and Mercy Otis Warren. He was born in Plymouth, 1764, and died in that town, 1828. His father had been speaker, 1787–1788, and his own service as clerk of the House extended from 1792 to 1802. During Shays's Rebellion he served upon the staff of Maj. Gen. Benjamin Lincoln with the rank of major, a title by which he was known in local circles. He was for many years collector of the port of Plymouth, and was the grandfather of Winslow Warren, at present collector of the port of Boston. It was voted by the General Court to place in this book a picture of Major Warren, but diligent search among his descendants fails to reveal any trace of a portrait in existence.

[2] The list is an honorable one, including the names of Harrison Gray Otis, Joseph Story, Josiah Quincy, Levi Lincoln, Charles Hale, Alexander H. Bullock, Harvey Jewell, John E. Sanford, John D. Long and John Q. A. Brackett. The senior surviving speaker is Daniel C. Eddy, who, a Baptist clergyman of Lowell, presided over the so-called Know Nothing House of 1855. He now resides in Brooklyn, N. Y. Two of our most distinguished speakers, Robert C. Winthrop and Nathaniel P. Banks, Jr., became equally noted presiding officers over the National House of Representatives, and both died in the fall of 1894.

and Boston, twenty years in all, between 1790 and 1821, was at different periods speaker eleven years. Famous men have been received in this hall. What a royal welcome was extended in 1817 to James Monroe, who, the president of the country, had been a valiant soldier during the Revolution. How the banquet in Doric Hall must have made the arches ring with the plaudits of those who greeted him! June 24, 1833, came Andrew Jackson, with his cabinet, including the subsequent president, Martin Van Buren; and, though it was in the recess of the Legislature, there was no lacking in the reception accorded to Old Hickory. This time the party was refreshed in the Senate chamber. John Tyler and his cabinet were here in 1843, June 17. In 1847 came James K. Polk, June 30, and with him a man to be elected to the presidency in 1856, James Buchanan. Millard Fillmore was here in 1848, October, the fall of his vice-presidential canvass. Grant and his cabinet were greeted April 17, 1875. It was in 1867, June 24, that Andrew Johnson and his party came hither. Alexander H. Bullock was governor, and in his elegant manner he welcomed the not over-popular President, an act which a wit of the day

REPRESENTATIVES' HALL — January, 1856.
(Looking South.)
CHARLES A. PHELPS, Speaker.

called "wrestling back hold with all the governor's principles;" but when he addressed Secretary Seward there was no conflict of duty and sentiment. To Mr. Seward the governor said, "Massachusetts has repeatedly expressed to you her love and admiration." To which the great war secretary replied, beginning, "I derived my first lesson in human rights from Massachusetts. . . . It was from the lips of John Quincy Adams that those words came." The "Advertiser," commenting on this reception, said that the people were courteous but not enthusiastic.

Nor have our visitors been confined to national officers. Black Hawk and Keokuk with their tawny faces were here received Oct. 30, 1837, and Black Hawk replied to the party who addressed him; March 20, 1868, came Kit Carson with a band of Utes; and Davy Crockett [1] was

---

[1] In his "Tour to the North and Down East," Colonel Crockett says (pages 76, 77): "From the top of the State House I had a fine view of the city, and was quite amused to see the representation of a large codfish hung up in the House of Assembly, or General Court, as they call it, to remind them, either that they depended a good deal on it for food, or made money by the fisheries. This is quite natural to me, for at home I have at one end of my house the antlers of a noble buck and the heavy paws of a bear. . . . I return the officers in the State House my thanks for their civility. I can't remember all their names, and therefore I won't name any of them." This entry was for May 6, 1834, less than two years before he won death and immortality in defending the Alamo.

here May 6, 1834. Twice were honors paid to
Lafayette,[1] and here were heard the eloquent
words of Kossuth.[2] The Prince of Wales[3] has
reason to remember the appearance of this chamber, as has also the Grand Duke Alexis;[4] but
the line is endless.[5]

"Except the Lord build the house they labor
in vain that build it." On the 4th of July, 1795,

---

[1] On the 26th of August, 1824, by a vote of the Legislature, passed in
expectation of the hero's coming, Lafayette received the citizens of Massachusetts in Doric Hall. It is said that on this occasion the national standard for
the first time was displayed from the cupola. June 16, 1825, he was again
received in the Representative chamber, Gov. Levi Lincoln in the speaker's
chair. This was the day before the corner-stone laying at Bunker Hill, and
Webster's immortal speech.

[2] Kossuth was received at the State House, April 27, 1852; and again, the
next day, passing under an arch bearing the inscription, "There is a com-
munity in mankind's destiny," he met both branches of the Legislature in the
Representative chamber, Governor Boutwell presiding, Henry Wilson being
president of the Senate and Nathaniel P. Banks, Jr., speaker of the House.

[3] Albert Edward, Prince of Wales, Oct. 18, 1860.

[4] Grand Duke Alexis of Russia, Dec. 8, 1871.

[5] On the 10th of May, 1894, the Legislature greeted Frederick Douglass.
In a happy manner he responded, and referred to his first appearance in the
hall, more than fifty years before. In a letter bearing date Feb. 8, 1895, Mr.
Douglass said he could not give exact date, but was sure it was in 1842. Reference to the files of the "Liberator" brings out this statement for the evening of Jan. 27, 1842: "It was by far the largest annual meeting ever held by
the society. [The Massachusetts Anti-slavery.] Every spot in the hall was
densely filled, and apparently all present not members were friends." Among
the speakers was "Frederick Douglass, a fugitive from slavery." The foregoing refers to the adjourned meeting from Faneuil Hall to this chamber, leave
having been granted by the House.

WILLIAM S. ROBINSON.
Born Dec. 7, 1818; died March 11, 1876.
Clerk, 1862 — 1872.

the voice of Peter Thatcher was heard invoking
the Divine blessing on the enterprise of a new
State House, then advanced to the corner-stone
laying. From the old State House, the members
of the government with the selectmen of Boston
and Masonic bodies had marched to the Old
South Church, and there had heard an address
by George Blake, thence through Milk Street
and Liberty Square they had returned to State
and so to the Old State House again, whence,
under the escort of the Independent Fusileers,
they had proceeded along Main Street to Winter
and so to and across the Common to Governor
Hancock's Pasture, where fifteen white horses,
representing the States of the Union, had drawn
the corner-stone. It is said that where are now
Hancock, Myrtle and Mt. Vernon streets, there
was only a dreary, dismal waste, and there were
but three decent houses. Boston had but twenty-
five thousand inhabitants, all told, and Massachusetts, Maine included, numbered only three
hundred and seventy-five thousand. But their
new enterprise was well thought out, and the
man who was then governor was one of the most

noted figures in the national annals; and these
were the words of Samuel Adams, as with Paul
Revere he lays the stone: —

FELLOW CITIZENS : — The Representatives of
the people, in General Court assembled, did sol-
emnly resolve that an edifice be erected upon this
spot of ground for the purpose of holding the
public councils of the Commonwealth of Massachusetts. By the request of their agents and
commissioners I do now lay the corner-stone.
May the superstructure be raised even to the
top stone without any untoward accident, and
remain permanent as the everlasting mountains.
May the principles of our excellent Constitution,
founded in nature and in the rights of man, be
ably defended here. And may the same principles be deeply engraven on the hearts of all citizens, and there be fixed unimpaired and in full
vigor till time shall be no more.

It is interesting to note that the year which
marked the first move towards a new State House
was the one in which by legislative enactment the
American dollar supplanted the British pound,
though the appropriation for the new edifice was
in the old style. This year also a petition was
presented asking for the setting off of the district
of Maine as an independent State, — a measure

EDWARD HUTCHINSON ROBBINS.
Born Feb. 19, 1758; died Dec. 29, 1829.
Speaker, 1793 — 1802.   Member of Building Commission.

that did not succeed till 1820. How nearly two
hundred men could find room in the old Representatives' Hall on State Street is a never-failing
source of wonder to all who visit that ancient
and venerated room. With the troubles incident
to the Revolution well in the background the
legislators, with a purpose of bettering their condition, acted as follows: —

RESOLVE FOR BUILDING A NEW STATE HOUSE.

February 16, 1795.

Resolved, That Edward H. Robbins, Esq.,
Thomas Dawes, Esq., and Mr. Charles Bulfinch,
be and they are hereby appointed agents on the
part of the Commonwealth; and they, or the major
part of them, are hereby fully authorized and
empowered to erect, build and finish a new State
House for the accommodation of all the legislative
and executive branches of government, on a spot
of ground in Boston commonly called the Governor's Pasture, containing about two acres, more
or less, adjoining the late Governor Hancock's
garden, and belonging to the heirs of said Governor Hancock: *provided*, the town of Boston will,
at their expense, purchase and cause the same to
be conveyed in fee-simple to the Commonwealth;
that appearing the most preferable spot for that
purpose, on such plan and model as said agents,

with the approbation of the committee hereinafter
named, or the major part of them, shall adopt.

And be it further *Resolved*, That the sum of
eight thousand pounds be, and the same hereby
is granted, to be paid out of the treasury of the
Commonwealth to said agents by warrant from the
Governor, by and with the advice of Council, for
the purpose aforesaid; they to be accountable to
the Commonwealth for the same, on the settlement
of their accounts for the expenditures on said
building, or at any other time when called upon
by the General Court.

The gentlemen to whom was intrusted the task
of designing and building executed their work
from beginning to end with not a whisper of
reproach; and, in passing, a glance at these old-
time worthies is not out of place. Edward
Hutchinson Robbins of Milton was a man whose
word for nearly or quite half a century was law
to all his fellow townsmen. From attaining his
majority till his death there was little time when
he was not filling some position of public trust.
Nine years in all, or four in the old and five in
this chamber, he was speaker; from 1802 to 1806
he was lieutenant-governor; thus gaining the title
by which most Milton people knew him. From
his estate in the town of Calais, Me., near Lake

THOMAS DAWES.
Born Aug. 5, 1731 ; died Jan. 2, 1809.
Member of Building Commission.

West Maguerrawock, pretty close to the king's dominions, were obtained the large timbers that became the columns in front and rear of the new State House and in Doric Hall. It is worthy of note that we pass on, almost a hundred years, from Robbins the builder to that other Robbins[1] who, as last year's chairman of the committee on the State House, waged here his battle *royal* for its preservation.

Thomas Dawes had experienced the full measure of British hate; his house had been sacked during the foreign occupancy of Boston, and by the enemy he was called "Jonathan Smoothing Plane." He had been a member of the convention of 1780, but his addition to this commission was on account of his practical experience as a builder. In 1800, owing to the deaths of Governor Sumner and Lieutenant-Governor Gill, Mr. Dawes, then president of the council, became acting governor. He was made a deacon in the Old South Church in 1786, and so continued till his death in 1809. His body lies in King's Chapel burying ground.

---

[1] Royal Robbins, member of the House of Representatives from the Eleventh Suffolk District, 1893-1894.

As for Charles Bulfinch, in the language of
that famous epitaph of Sir Christopher Wren,
who designed St. Paul's Church, "If you seek
his monument, look around."

Such were the men who reared these walls,
and in the intervening years no words of criti-
cism have been uttered over their work. They
builded for the century, and now at its end we
look back along the way, passing in review some
of the scenes of which this chamber was the
theatre. Every Massachusetts signer of the Declaration of Independence save Hancock must have
seen this interior; some of the events here wit-
nessed were thrilling in their interest. Robert
Treat Paine was a member of the council in
1804, and so repeatedly entered here. Elbridge
Gerry, as governor in 1810-1812, took his oath
of office in this room. While we may have no
record of Samuel Adams in the chamber itself,
we well know his early part in building, and
we know that at the State House, Oct. 6, 1803,
was formed the procession which escorted his remains to their final resting place in the Granary
Burial Ground. Most impressive of all was when,
bowed with his four-score and five years, John

Adams came hither to take his seat as a member
of the Constitutional Convention of 1820. Con-
scious of his infirmities, he had declined the high
honor of presiding officer to which the delegates
had elected him, but to a man those delegates
of seventy-five years ago rose and with uncovered heads saluted the foremost citizen of Massachusetts as he was escorted to his permanent
seat at the right of the president. Though he
was not a frequent speaker in that body, yet his
voice and vote are on record, and they make a
part of the chain linking us with that past of
which the Adamses, Hancock, Otis and Revere
were so considerable a part. Still closer binding
us to the history that we venerate, in this room,
Feb. 8, 1800, Fisher Ames gave his eulogy on
Washington, a task for which he was peculiarly
well fitted, having given the address to Congress
when Washington retired from the presidency.
And in later days there were giants who wrestled
here. Daniel Webster had been a citizen of this
Commonwealth only four years when he was sent,
in 1820, to assist in revising the Constitution.
Here, as everywhere, his voice was potent, and
in the light of the events of to-day it is a pleas-

ure to find that he uttered this protest against
vast accumulations of wealth: "The history of
other nations may teach us how favorable to public liberty is the division of the soil into small
freeholds: and a system of laws of which the
tendency is without violence or injustice to pro-
duce and to preserve a degree of equality of
property. . . . The freest government, if it could
exist, would not long be acceptable if the tendency of the laws were to create a rapid accumu-
lation of property in a few hands and to render
the great mass of the population dependent and
penniless." In 1888, from the 14th to the 19th
of July, Ex-President Hayes presided in this
hall, with all the grace so characteristic of him,
over the sessions of the Prison Congress, and in
his address uttered words which should link his
name with those of John Howard and Dorothea
Dix: "But the citizen cannot be loyal to his
country and faithful to her true significance if he
neglects the children of misfortune, of poverty, of
weakness and of wickedness, who are, or who are
in danger of being, enrolled in the ranks of crime.
From the earliest dawn of human life it has been

an irrepealable condition of its existence that all
men are indeed their brothers' keepers."

The year 1858 beheld here one of the most
remarkable events in our history. Prompted by
Garrison, Phillips and others of the anti-slavery
leaders, the Legislature projected the removal
of Edward Greeley Loring, judge of probate in
Suffolk County, for alleged malfeasance in the
rendition of Anthony Burns. Caleb Cushing,
dividing the leadership of the Massachusetts bar
with Rufus Choate, defended the accused in a
manner worthy of his experience and name. It
was the first and only year of John A. Andrew
in the Legislature. A confessed abolitionist, his
reputation up to that time was purely local, but
so determined, so masterly was his action that
the obnoxious officer was removed, and the work
of the Representative made him the successor of
Nathaniel P. Banks, Jr., in the gubernatorial chair.[1]

It was near the close of the session of 1885
that the very depths were stirred over the Boston

---

[1] Among those who struggled with Andrew for what he considered good
government was Geo. D. Wells, a young lawyer from Greenfield, who fell Oct.
13, 1864, colonel of the Thirty-fourth Massachusetts, at Stickney Farm, Va.,
a prelude to the battle of Cedar Creek. Many others who here helped make
laws, later went forth to defend them.

police bill. Victors and vanquished fought long and well. All the devices possible to skilled parliamentarians had only put off the inevitable end. Confusion reigned almost supreme. The speaker had threatened to name recalcitrant members; they in turn had invoked direst vengeance on any officer who should lay violent hands upon them. Gavels, many, were broken in a vain effort to maintain order, and as a last resort a carpenter's hammer had been secured, to be used should the last gavel be destroyed. But Speaker J. Q. A. Brackett held firmly to his post, and with the vote and the disappearance of the beaten came peace and order.

In this address I have in the main confined myself to this room, but were we to go beyond its bounds, matters of interest would be found on every hand.[1]   In Doric Hall, just beneath us, was

---

[1] "If the dome were gilded, it is said by those of artistic and travel-improved taste, it would equal in beauty any public building in Europe. The cost of such improvement would be $5,500. It would last without protection ten years, and might be made to stand for a longer term. No other equivalent improvement of the Capitol could be effected by so slight an expense." (Governor Banks's valedictory, 1851.)

The resolve under which the gilding was first done bears date of June 25, 1874. For painting the outside of the State House and for gilding the dome Cyrus T. Clark was paid $8,200.94. The dome was re-gilded in 1888, at a cost of $4,758.79; the first gilding outlasting the governor's estimate by four years.

REPRESENTATIVES' HALL.—Jan. 2, 1895.

(Looking South.)

organized the first volunteer company in the war of the rebellion, and doorkeeper John Kinnear, over there, was a member. How many thousands of our citizens climbed the steps leading to the hall to look finally on the faces of Sumner and Wilson when their remains there lay in state? How many flags were in that space or in front of the capitol intrusted to the care and keeping of departing regiments, and on their return this same hall became their final resting place? Representatives from every war waged by the United States have served in this room, and in the last House there were thirty-four veterans of the latest strife. In the present body there are thirty-six.

What is to be the fate of this building and of this room? There are those who exclaim, "Raze it, raze it!" but out from the hearts of the masses of our citizens comes the cry, "Save it, save it!" All sorts of imaginary ills are found in and about these walls, evils not dreamed of till their destruction was sought. The same iconoclastic spirit, extant a thousand years ago, would have found the pyramids of Egypt not fireproof and Pompey's pillar out of plumb. Destroying them, there had been no forty centuries to look down upon Napo-

leon's soldiers, prompting them to prodigies of
valor, nor had the names of Frenchmen, slain
in the siege of Alexandria, been graven on the
base of that famous shaft. We are told that,
because the years after the revolution to those
of the rebellion were days of peace, there could
little interest attach to these walls; but if the
presence and spirit of Andrew and of those who
here held their ground in storm and sunshine do
not render these walls sacred for all time, then let
us remember that Whittier, one of our predecessors, sang the praises of peace, saying, —

> " Peace hath higher tests of manhood
> Than battles ever knew."

"But what shall we do with it?" is the refrain.
Let it be the Massachusetts forum. Let mankind
hither come and here discuss their grievances, if
such they be. Many of us recall that day of last
year when the thousands of unemployed surged
up from the Common, up the stairways leading
to this room, and how they beat upon these doors,
seeking help for their distresses; and we recall
how in their spirit of violence they were met by
the firm hand of the governor and faced about

and driven out. To be sure they did later come to this very room and here present and plead their cause; but suppose this chamber, with all its mighty memories, had been open to them, and that in this place they could then have told their woes, who can say that the effect would not be for good? If here men should learn to make war no more, then God be praised. What better place can be found, the world over, where men may beat their swords into ploughshares and their spears into pruning hooks? In a sense it has already been a forum for the people, since within this space have rung out the most eloquent voices of the State and nation. Their principles prevented Garrison and Phillips being members of this body, but at legislative hearings, again and again, have their words been heard in behalf of what they deemed the truth. More than fifty years since the matchless voice of Lucy Stone was heard here, pouring out her heart for the enfranchisement of woman; and to hers in later years have been joined those of Julia Ward Howe and Mary A. Livermore, making a peerless trio for God and the right.

Annually more than fifty thousand people

climb the one hundred and seventy steps leading to the lantern whence is had the most
glorious view afforded by western civilization.
Above still shines the pine cone, a source of
pride to the builders, calling to mind the remote
district of Maine, yet once a distinct part of the
Commonwealth; and, though many may see in
it resemblance to other objects than the cone, yet
it is dear to the hearts of all, as cherished as to
the Englishman is the golden grasshopper which
at the pinnacle of the tower of London's Royal
Exchange has long stayed his aerial flight.

And to-day the last legislative act in this chamber is had. The story of a century is told.

Then, grand old hall, hallowed by the presence
and words of thy many, many thousands, with all
thy memories, all thy glory, hail and farewell!

NOTE. — There is a wide difference in the quality of illustrations in this book. A half-tone cannot be better than the
picture from which it is made. A good photograph makes a
good engraving. The securing of the originals of some of these
portraits was a serious task. The faces of Governor SUMNER,
Speaker ROBBINS, Commissioner DAWES and Architect BUL-
FINCH were copied from illustrations in books belonging to the
State Library. Lieutenant-Governor GILL's picture is from a
photograph belonging to his great-grandson, F. W. GILL of

ALFRED S. ROE.
Representative, 16th Worcester District.

Boston. The orginal oil painting (possibly a Stuart) is in the possession of some branch of the Boylston family, in which the lieutenant-governor found his second wife. Speaker Banks's picture is from a daguerreotype made contemporaneously by J. J. Hawes of Tremont Row; that of Robert C. Winthrop is also from an early source. Messenger Kuhn's face is had from a copy of an oil painting in the possession of the Sergeant-at-Arms. Speaker Meyer's portrait is made from a photograph of a recent oil painting by Julian Story. The earlier views of the Hall are from wood cuts in Gleason's and Ballou's Pictorials.

In conclusion, it is only fair that I should acknowledge my obligations to State Librarian C. B. Tillinghast, whose suggestions and favors have contributed much to the details of this paper, and also to the State Printers, whose care and taste have resulted in making this volume a fine specimen of the book-maker's art. — A. S. R.

APPENDIX.

EXECUTIVE AND LEGISLATIVE
DEPARTMENTS OF THE GOVERNMENT

OF THE

Commonwealth of Massachusetts.

1895.

EXECUTIVE DEPARTMENT.

--- • ---

SENATE.

PRESIDENT:

Hon. WILLIAM M. BUTLER, . New Bedford.

CLERK:

HENRY D. COOLIDGE, . . C .

ASSISTANT CLERK:

WILLIAM H. SANGER, . b .

NAME.	ADDRESS.	DISTRICT.
Atherton, Horace H.,	Saugus,	Fifth Essex.
Atwood, Edward B.,	Plymouth,	First Plymouth.
Bessom, Eugene A.,	Lynn,	First Essex.
Bill, Ledyard,	Paxton,	Third Worcester.
Blodgett, Percival,	Templeton,	Worcester and Hampshire.
Bradford, Edward S.,	Springfield,	First Hampden.
Burns, George J.,	Ayer,	Fifth Middlesex.
Butler, William M.,	New Bedford,	Third Bristol.
Corbett, Joseph J.,	Boston,	Second Suffolk.
Darling, Francis W.,	Hyde Park,	First Norfolk.
Durant, William B.,	Cambridge,	Third Middlesex.
Foss, Ether S.,	Lowell,	Seventh Middlesex.
Frothingham, Edward G.,	Haverhill,	Fourth Essex.
Fuller, Granville A.,	Boston,	Eighth Suffolk.
Gage, George L.,	Lawrence,	Sixth Essex.

SENATE – Concluded.

NAME.	ADDRESS.	DISTRICT.
Galloupe, George A.,	Beverly,	Second Essex.
Gilbride, Michael B.,	Boston,	Third Suffolk.
Gray, Robert S.,	Walpole,	Second Norfolk.
Harvey, Edwin B.,	Westborough,	Second Worcester.
Hutchinson, Isaac P.,	Boston,	Seventh Suffolk.
Lawrence, George P.,	North Adams,	Berkshire.
Leach, James C.,	Bridgewater,	Second Plymouth.
Maccabe, Joseph B.,	Boston,	First Suffolk.
Malone, Dana,	Greenfield,	Franklin.
McMorrow, William H.,	Boston,	Sixth Suffolk.
Miller, Joel D.,	Leominster,	Fourth Worcester.
Morse, William A.,	Tisbury,	Cape.
Neill, Joseph O.,	Fall River,	Second Bristol.
Niles, James P.,	Watertown,	Second Middlesex.
Perkins, George W.,	Somerville,	First Middlesex.
Quinn, John, Jr.,	Boston,	Fourth Suffolk.
Reed, George A.,	Framingham,	Fourth Middlesex.
Ripley, John B.,	Chester,	{ Berkshire and Hampshire. }
Salisbury, Stephen,	Worcester,	First Worcester.
Sanger, George P.,	Boston,	Fifth Suffolk.
Smith, Sylvanus,	Gloucester,	Third Essex.
Southard, Louis C.,	Easton,	First Bristol.
Sprague, Charles F.,	Boston,	Ninth Suffolk.
Wellman, Arthur H.,	Malden,	Sixth Middlesex.
Whitcomb, Marciene H.,	Holyoke,	Second Hampden.

HOUSE OF REPRESENTATIVES.

HON. GEORGE V. L. MEYER, . . Boston.

CLERK.

ELIHU A. McLAUGHLIN, Boston.

ASSISTANT CLERK.

JAMES M. KIMBALL, Lynn.

NAME.	DISTRICT.	ADDRESS.
Allen, Daniel W., .	19, Essex,	Lynn.
Allen, Romeo E.,	12, Worcester	Shrewsbury.
Atsatt, Isaiah P., .	7. Plymouth,	Mattapoisett.
Austin, Frederick E.,	3, Bristol, .	Taunton.
Bailey, George W., .	4, Berkshire,	Pittsfield.
Bailey, James A., Jr.,	15, Middlesex,	Arlington.
Baker, Theophilus B., .	2, Barnstable,	Harwich.
Balch, Charles T., .	7, Essex,	Groveland.
Bancroft, Charles G.,	13, Worcester,	Clinton.
Bancroft, Solon, .	11, Middlesex,	Reading.
Barber, Harding R.,	1, Worcester,	Athol.
Barker, Albert F., .	3, Plymouth,	Hanson.
Barnes, Erwin F., .	6, Berkshire,	West Stockbridge.
Barnes, Franklin O.,	26, Suffolk, .	Chelsea.

HOUSE OF REPRESENTATIVES—CONTINUED.

NAME.	DISTRICT.	ADDRESS.
Barry, Daniel J ,	11, Suffolk,	Boston.
Bates, John L.,	1, Suffolk,	Boston.
Beaman, Algernon T.,	4, Worcester,	Princeton.
Bennett, Frank S.,*	24, Middlesex,	Tyngsborough.
Bird, George B.,	24, Suffolk,	Boston.
Bliss, Henry C.,	2, Hampden,	West Springfield.
Blodgett, Benjamin F.,	5, Worcester,	West Brookfield.
Bond, Charles P.,	18, Middlesex,	Waltham.
Bourne, Samuel S.,	8, Plymouth,	Middleborough.
Boutwell, Harvey L.,	9, Middlesex,	Malden.
Bradford, Fred. H.,	18, Middlesex,	Waltham.
Bradley, Manassah E.,	2, Suffolk,	Boston.
Brown, Charles D.,	10, Essex,	Gloucester.
Brown, Frederick A.,	8, Worcester,	Webster.
Bullock, Benjamin S.,	10, Essex,	Manchester.
Burges, William H.,	2, Plymouth,	Kingston.
Burt, J. Marshall,	9, Hampden,	East Longmeadow.
Burt, T. Preston,	3, Bristol,	Taunton.
Carroll, Charles W.,	11, Worcester,	Milford.
Carter, William,	9, Norfolk,	Needham.
Casey, Daniel C.,	20, Suffolk,	Boston.
Chandler, Frank,	16, Middlesex,	Belmont.
Clark, Luther W.,	4, Franklin,	Deerfield.
Cochran, James A.,	1, Suffolk,	Boston.
Collins, Michael W.,	3, Suffolk,	Boston.
Cook, Heman S.,	3, Barnstable,	Provincetown.
Cook, Gilbert, †	11, Worcester,	Lunenburg.

* Died April 10.   † Died February 17.

HOUSE OF REPRESENTATIVES—CONTINUED

NAME.	DISTRICT.	ADDRESS.
Creed, James F.,	15, Suffolk,	Boston.
Crane, Ellery B.,*	21, Worcester,	Worcester.
Dallinger, Frederick W.,	2, Middlesex,	Cambridge.
Davis, William W.,	21, Suffolk,	Boston.
Denham, Thomas M.,	5, Bristol,	New Bedford.
Dickinson, David T.,	1, Middlesex,	Cambridge.
Donahue, Thomas,	8, Bristol,	Fall River.
Donovan, Timothy J.,	4, Suffolk,	Boston.
Donovan, William F.,	8, Suffolk,	Boston.
Donovan, William J.,	2, Suffolk,	Boston.
Dow, Harry R.,	5, Essex,	Lawrence.
Drew, William H.,	1, Plymouth,	Plymouth.
Driscoll, Daniel M.,	12, Suffolk,	Boston.
Driscoll, William P.,	12, Suffolk,	Boston.
Drury, Levi A.,	3, Essex,	Bradford.
Duddy, Robert,	7, Middlesex,	Somerville.
Eddy, George M.,	6, Bristol,	New Bedford.
Edgarton, Henry,	32, Middlesex,	Shirley.
Edgerton, Albert H.,	5, Worcester,	Sturbridge.
Eldredge, Alpheus M.,	11, Plymouth,	Brockton.
Estes, Benjamin F.,	19, Essex,	Lynn.
Fallon, Thomas F.,	19, Suffolk,	Boston.
Ferson, Clarentine E.,	15, Worcester,	Fitchburg.
Fillmore, Wellington,	2, Middlesex,	Cambridge.
Fisk, Henry H.,	1, Barnstable,	Dennis.
Flint, James H.,	5, Norfolk,	Weymouth.
Flint, Silas W.,	13, Middlesex,	Wakefield.

* Elected to succeed Henry Y. Simpson, deceased.

HOUSE OF REPRESENTATIVES—CONTINUED.

NAME.	DISTRICT.	ADDRESS.
Flynn, Joseph J.,	4, Essex,	Lawrence.
Foote, William H.,	2, Hampden,	Westfield.
Ford, William E.,	23, Suffolk,	Boston.
Foss, Otis,	1, Dukes,	Cottage City.
Fowle, George F.,	14, Middlesex,	Woburn.
French, Zenas A.,	6, Norfolk,	Holbrook.
Gallivan, James A.,	13, Suffolk,	Boston.
Gardner, John J.,	1, Nantucket,	Nantucket.
Gauss, John D. H.,	13, Essex,	Salem.
Gaylord, Henry E.,	3, Hampshire,	South Hadley.
Geary, Michael P.,	13, Suffolk,	Boston.
George, Samuel W.,	2, Essex,	Haverhill.
Gillingham, James L.,	4, Bristol,	Fairhaven.
Goodrich, Charles W.,	3, Berkshire,	Hinsdale.
Graham, William T.,	5, Suffolk,	Boston.
Grant, Alexander,	5, Hampden,	Chicopee.
Gray, Joshua S.,	5, Plymouth,	Rockland.
Greenwood, Abner,	27, Middlesex,	Ashland.
Grover, Thomas E.,	4, Norfolk,	Canton.
Hale, Edward A.,	8, Essex,	Newburyport.
Hammond, Charles L.,	5, Norfolk,	Quincy.
Hammond, George,	7, Worcester,	Charlton.
Harlow, Franklin P.,	6, Plymouth,	Whitman.
Harrington, James L.,*	14, Worcester,	Lunenburg.
Harvey, Benjamin C.,	8, Hampden,	Springfield.
Harwood, Albert L.,	17, Middlesex,	Newton Centre.
Hastings, Samuel,	2, Franklin,	Warwick.

* Elected to succeed Gilbert Cook, deceased.

HOUSE OF REPRESENTATIVES — CONTINUED.

NAME.	DISTRICT.	ADDRESS.
Hathaway, Bowers C.,	12, Worcester,	Westborough.
Hathaway, Frederic W.,	12, Plymouth,	Brockton.
Hawkes, Wesley O.,	31, Middlesex,	Westford.
Hayes, William H. I.,	24, Middlesex,	Lowell.
Hibbard, George A.,	18, Suffolk,	Boston.
Higgins, Sumner C.,	4, Middlesex,	Cambridge.
Hoban, Thomas F.,	25, Middlesex,	Lowell.
Holden, Joshua B.,	11, Suffolk,	Boston.
Holland, Timothy,	19, Suffolk,	Boston.
Hollis, J. Edward,	17, Middlesex,	Newton.
Holt, E. Clarence,	3, Bristol,	Taunton.
Horan, John G.,	15, Suffolk,	Boston.
Howe, Louis P.,	29, Middlesex,	Marlborough.
Humphrey, Henry D.,	1, Norfolk,	Dedham.
Huse, Caleb B.,	8, Essex,	Newburyport.
Hutchinson, W. Henry,	20, Essex,	Lynn.
Irwin, Richard W.,	1, Hampshire,	Northampton.
Ives, Dwight H.,	3, Hampden,	Holyoke.
Jenks, William S.,	2, Berkshire,	Adams.
Johnson, Edward P.,	18, Essex,	Lynn.
Jones, George R.,	11, Middlesex,	Melrose.
Jordan, Cyrus A.,	14, Essex,	Salem.
Jourdan, Benjamin A.,	10, Worcester,	Upton.
Kaan, Frank W.,	6, Middlesex,	Somerville.
Keenan, James,	16, Suffolk,	Boston.
Keenan, Thomas F.,	8, Suffolk,	Boston.
Kellogg, John E.,	15, Worcester,	Fitchburg.

House of Representatives—Continued.

NAME.	DISTRICT.	ADDRESS.
Kimball, William G.,	2, Hampshire,	Huntington.
Kingman, Francis M.,	9, Plymouth,	East Bridgewater.
Knox, Joseph B.,	22, Worcester,	Worcester.
Krebbs, Franz H., Jr.,	17, Suffolk,	Boston.
Lawrence, Amos A.,	4, Plymouth,	Cohasset.
Leach, George A.,	28, Middlesex,	Wayland.
Leach, Osgood L.,	3, Franklin,	Northfield.
Leach, Warren S.,	2, Bristol,	Raynham.
Light, Charles F.,	3, Norfolk,	Hyde Park.
Lowell, Francis C.,	11, Suffolk,	Boston.
Lynch, John M.,	4, Essex,	Lawrence.
Macomber, John A., 2d,	7, Bristol,	Westport.
Mann, Hugo,	5, Franklin,	Buckland.
Marden, William H.,	12, Middlesex,	Stoneham.
Mayo, Samuel N.,	8, Middlesex,	Medford.
McCarthy, Jeremiah J.,	4, Suffolk,	Boston.
McMackin, Bernard,	7, Suffolk,	Boston.
Melaven, James F.,	20, Worcester,	Worcester.
Mellen, George H.,	23, Worcester,	Worcester.
Mellen, James H.,	19, Worcester,	Worcester.
Meyer, George v. L.,	9, Suffolk,	Boston.
Mills, Charles E.,	9, Bristol,	Fall River.
Mitchell, Samuel H.,	25, Suffolk,	Boston.
Mooney, Joseph F.,	8, Bristol,	Fall River.
Moore, E. Lewis,	28, Middlesex,	Framingham.
Moran, William,	8, Bristol,	Fall River.
Moriarty, Eugene M.,	18, Worcester,	Worcester.

HOUSE OF REPRESENTATIVES—CONTINUED.

NAME.	DISTRICT.	ADDRESS.
Mulvey, Mark B.,	22, Suffolk,	Boston.
Murphy, Timothy F.,	7, Suffolk,	Boston.
Myers, James J.,	1, Middlesex,	Cambridge.
Newell, Herbert,	1, Franklin,	Shelburne.
Newell, Richard,	1, Essex,	West Newbury.
Newhall, George H.,	17, Essex,	Lynn.
Newhall, John B.,	18, Essex,	Lynn.
Norton, Joseph J.,	11, Suffolk,	Boston.
O'Brien, Michael J.,	5, Suffolk,	Boston.
O'Connor, John J.,	23, Middlesex,	Lowell.
O'Hara, John M.,	3, Suffolk,	Boston.
Osgood, L. Edgar,	6, Essex,	North Andover.
Parker, Theodore K.,	2, Worcester,	Winchendon.
Penniman, George W.,	10, Plymouth,	Brockton.
Perkins, Lyman H.,	6, Hampden,	Springfield.
Phelps, Carlton T.,	1, Berkshire,	North Adams.
Pinkham, Edward W.,	17, Essex,	Lynn.
Porter, Burrill, Jr.,	1, Bristol,	No. Attleborough.
Porter, George W.,	7, Norfolk,	Avon.
Porter, J. Frank,	22, Essex,	Danvers.
Prevaux, John J.,	1, Essex,	Amesbury.
Putnam, George E.,	22, Middlesex,	Lowell.
Quint, Nicolas M.,	21, Essex,	Peabody.
Quirk, Charles I.,	20, Suffolk,	Boston.
Rice, Henry F.,	9, Worcester,	Sutton.
Richardson, Robert A.,	3, Essex,	Haverhill.
Roberts, Ernest W.,	27, Suffolk,	Chelsea.

HOUSE OF REPRESENTATIVES—CONTINUED.

NAME.	DISTRICT.	ADDRESS.
Roe, Alfred S.,	16, Worcester,	Worcester.
Root, Silas B.,	1, Hampden,	Granville.
Roper, George A.,	24, Middlesex,	Lowell.
Ross, Samuel,	5, Bristol,	New Bedford.
Rourke, Daniel D.,	6, Suffolk,	Boston.
Rourke, Fred H.,	21, Middlesex,	Lowell.
Russell, George G.,	15, Essex,	Salem.
Ryan, James F.,	16, Suffolk,	Boston.
Ryder, Martin F.,	6, Suffolk,	Boston.
Sargent, Charles F.,	5, Essex,	Lawrence.
Seates, George M.,	21, Suffolk,	Boston.
Searls, William P.,	17, Worcester,	Worcester.
Shea, John T.,	3, Middlesex,	Cambridge.
Sheehan, John F.,	4, Hampden,	Holyoke.
Shepherd, William,	20, Essex,	Lynn.
Sibley, Frank M.,	5, Hampshire,	Ware.
Sisson, Henry D.,	7, Berkshire,	New Marlborough.
Slade, David F.,	9, Bristol,	Fall River.
Sleeper, George T.,	27, Suffolk,	Winthrop.
Smith, Albert C.,	18, Suffolk,	Boston.
Smith, Henry M.,	5, Berkshire,	Lee.
Snow, George F.,	20, Middlesex,	Chelmsford.
Southworth, Amasa E.,	5, Middlesex,	Somerville.
Spalding, Warren F.,	4, Middlesex,	Cambridge.
Spofford, John C.,	10, Middlesex,	Everett.
Spring, Arthur L.,	10, Suffolk,	Boston.
Stanley, Fred D.,	6, Bristol,	New Bedford.

HOUSE OF REPRESENTATIVES—CONTINUED.

NAME.	DISTRICT.	ADDRESS.
Stevens, Ezra A.,	9, Middlesex,	Malden.
St. John, Thomas E.,	2, Essex,	Haverhill.
Stocker, Joseph W.,	12, Essex,	Beverly.
Stone, Daniel D.,	9, Essex,	Hamilton.
Strong, Homer O.,	1, Hampshire,	Southampton.
Sturtevant, Charles F.,	23, Suffolk,	Boston.
Tarr, George J.,	10, Essex,	Gloucester.
Teamoh, Robert T.,	9, Suffolk,	Boston.
Thacher, Josiah P.,	30, Middlesex,	Littleton.
Thurston, Lyman D.,	6, Worcester,	Leicester.
Tolman, William,	1, Berkshire,	Pittsfield.
Tower, Henry,	29, Middlesex,	Hudson.
Towle, William W.,	17, Suffolk,	Boston.
Tuite, Michael,	11, Worcester,	Blackstone.
Turner, Arthur H.,	13, Worcester,	Harvard.
Turner, George W.,*	6, Hampden,	Springfield.
Tuttle, John E.,	24, Suffolk,	Boston.
Utley, Charles H.,	2, Norfolk,	Brookline.
Wadden, Frank L.,	16, Essex,	Marblehead.
Waite, Gilman,	2, Worcester,	Templeton.
Wakefield, Charles E.,	1, Hampshire,	Amherst.
Wales, George A.,	7, Norfolk,	Stoughton.
Wallis, Horace E.,	10, Hampden,	Holland.
Warriner, Stephen C.,	8, Hampden,	Springfield.
Waterman, George B.,	1, Berkshire,	Williamstown.
Wentworth, George L.,	5, Norfolk,	Weymouth.
Weston, Clarence P.,	10, Suffolk,	Boston.

* Elected to succeed Joseph L. Shipley, deceased.

HOUSE OF REPRESENTATIVES – CONCLUDED.

NAME.	DISTRICT.	ADDRESS.
Wheaton, Mark O.,	1, Bristol,	Attleborough.
Whitaker, Elbridge J.,	8, Norfolk,	Wrentham.
White, George E.,	1, Barnstable,	Sandwich.
White, William S,	8, Norfolk,	Foxborough.
Wiley, Albert L.,	3, Worcester,	Hardwick.
Willard, Edward E.,	26, Suffolk,	Chelsea.
Wilson, Edward H.,	26, Middlesex,	Natick.
Winn, John,	19, Middlesex,	Woburn.
Wood, Henry O.,	10, Bristol,	Swanzey.
Woodfall, J. Loring,	11, Essex,	Rockport.
Young, Charles L.,	7, Hampden,	Springfield.

www.ingramcontent.com/pod-product-compliance
Lightning Source LLC
Chambersburg PA
CBHW030629270326
41927CB00007B/1367